Brain Power.

How to Track and Kill your Enemies.

Advanced Electromagnetic Waves Warfare

We are against wars that kill innocent women and children.

We will do anything to bring perpetrators to justice.
David Gomadza

The First Global President of the World

www.twofuture.world

PAPERBACK ISBN: 9798874314118

DEDICATION

We are against wars that kill innocent women and children. Will do anything to bring perpetrators to justice.
How to track and kill your enemies.

TABLE OF CONTENTS

THE SOLUTION

1. Make a list of all your enemies according to priority.
2. Google their pictures of when they were young and old and one a very recent one. You need three photos.
3. Just think of the number …
4. You will hear the message:
    Hi, this is...
    How can I help you?
5. Say I want to clone someone.
You will get a question:
Do you have their picture with you?
You will be asked to look in their eyes.
What do you want to do with them?
Blast them for killing innocent women and children.
You will hear the message:
Do you know code 620? Silently in your head say 620.
If you are one of a few men with DNA sequence 620 that say in wars women are collateral, then you will hear the message.

620 Whenatwarwomenarecollateral.start
CCAATTAAGGGG for men

When at war women are collateral
You will then be asked to repeat a few lines to correct this DNA sequence code first before you start pointing fingers at others.

Start by thinking [saying silently in your brain]
"My voice is my password.
Men say
GGAATTGGAAGGG
GGAAGGTTGGGGG
Space out
End

Out
Save
Endorse now
Space in
Start.end
Permanent save

For women think silently or say silently
GGTTAAGGAACCC
Space out
End
Out
Save
Endorse
Now
Space in
Start.end
Permanent save

Once that is done then we can proceed.
We will check this person killing women and children to make
sure that he does not have this DNA sequence also.
If he has this DNA sequence and if your grievances relate to
the killings of women and children, then you might want to
reconsider other options.
Not because it is an excuse everyone knows that killing
women and children is against all of us.
We as Tomorrow's World Order, the death of a child or a
woman is an attack on all of us.

But there are cases where some regimes are deliberately
altering DNA sequences to boost their causes of harvesting
souls.
Once we are satisfied, we will then approve the cloning of that
person.
We will do further checks and send the clone once we are
satisfied that we want the person as well.

6. We will clone that person. We will send you that clone.

This is how to use the clone to locate that person.

Download one of our video's links at the end

The Identifier & the Tracker.

This video will tell you the number assigned to your clone,
usually a 10-digit starting with 78 is a man and 72 if it is a
woman.

Download video two the assigner see link at the end.

The Assigner

This video is to send to the person with your instructions. You
can secret or pass your message. Normally if in silent mode
then the person might not know because the clone is himself
and he might have Jeda vu experience but will not know
anything.
But the one with the message will make him aware.

Send with commands.

Create.message

Convert my brain thoughts into nerve impulses and use an
unlock key to reveal on arrival.
[Then start thinking what you want to say]
For example: I stand today as the judge of Tomorrow's World
Order, and we have found you guilty of crimes against
humanity as a whole mainly against women and children. We
regard the death of a child or woman as an attack on all of us.
As such we are here delivering our message to you that you
must face our best snipers, or a borrowed drone armed with
explosives.

send.end
start
start.end
send

Now say the number of the clone you obtained using the above video the identifier and tracker starting with 78 or 72 mainly a 10-digit number. Write commands to send it.

send.clone [78.......]tooriginalattachabovemessage.start

That means send clone 78… to original attach above message .start

Just know after this the person might start moving if he was in a fixed position.

How the clone will act.

The clone will locate the original person. This is because when one looked in the eyes of this person our system will have identified him and assigned all the information. Our geo-body location system will have collected all the information needed to locate this person. All one must do is to assign the clone to do a task by going to its original person.
The clone will do and when it arrives will simply enter its owner depositing the message as nerve impulses that are converted to action potential thereby delivering the message as the message instantly becomes that person's brain thoughts.
For most of the first time they will not notice that they have just received a clone of themselves. The effect of the clone is to override the current brain thoughts with a bit of a stuck mode and a Jeda vu.
Whatever you command through programming the clone is what the original person will do at least for a few minutes until he realizes that there is a problem as the brain might get stuck for a few seconds as what he was thinking at that time is not

finally processed.
The brain when thinking produces a lot of actions that must complete a full cycle. The arrival of the clone will interfere with the current brain sequence.

Arrival of the clone.

Once the clone has arrived you must also command the clone to send you a key once the message has been opened using this command.

Once opened send back the key.[me]
Where me is your assigned number the time you requested a clone.
After delivering the message and returning to its owner the clone becomes one again with the owner.

Once delivery has been received on our side, we will undo the cloning after getting the coordinates of the person. You will also receive the coordinates through the locator video.

The Locator.

Simply play this video; the locator to know exactly where the person is at the time.
You must know that since everything is based on our reading of the brain, we use Yahweh's time, which means each hour has 1 hour and 90 minutes.

Yahweh's time 23:90 minutes

The brain uses Yahweh's time 23:90 meaning that it will save every activity after 30 minutes of normal human time.
That means if normal human time occurred at 17.21 our books and files will show the time as 17.51.
There is no mistake if actual time differs with the time on the report just adjust by half an hour.

The locator is a video you simply play to get the coordinates of
what the person is doing.
You can also download the brain and activity reader video to
play at the same time to know exactly what that person is
doing at that time.

The Brain Reader and Activity Reader

This video must be played at the same time as the locater
video. This will narrate exactly word for word what the person
is doing; telling you exactly his feelings, what he is doing, any
instruments he or she is using, thinking, his nerve impulses
and all his surroundings to know exactly the situation.

I DECODED THE BRAIN PLAY THIS VIDEO A DIGITAL
BRAIN READER ANALOGUE visit www.twofuture.world

https://www.youtube.com/watch?v=rmBSVmwKwR0&t=266s

You can also get this video; the Digital Analogue Thoughts to
Words converter and play at the same time to know exactly
what your enemy is thinking word to word.

A Digital Thoughts to Words Converter

https://www.youtube.com/watch?v=i5KCRpKqmqY&t=645s

How to communicate with your enemy.

You can communicate with your enemy. You must first, before
sending the clone, command the clone to hide after entering
the original person and after delivering the message.
You can add a command like.

Hideinthenavalonarrival.start

That means hide in the navel on arrival

That also means before sending the clone you must have
cloned the person twice.
You then command one of the clones to hide in your own
naval but for that time only if you carry someone in your naval
that person might know then you become the target.

Commands the first clone, the one to hide in your naval.

Jumpinto[me]andhideinthenaval.start

This meaning jump into [me] where me is your number
assigned at the beginning and hide in the navel .start

The clone will jump into you and hide in the naval.

Commands to the second clone are the ones we discussed
above.

How to communicate

You can send commands as well to initiate talks with the
enemy.
After delivering message the

ifyouhearnavalvibrationsalertoriginalperson.start

if you hear naval vibrations alert original person .start

How you communicate with the enemy.

Press the naval with the index finger to initiate vibrations.

The person on the other end will answer the vibrations.
Now start the communications.

Communication.sign-in
Hello

After finishing then say
Communication.sign-out

This is for those who want to end up putting a trail on the person.

If negotiations have failed, then you can take it further.
Unless the person is advanced as well, he might not know that
now you are like a heat seeking missile.

We do not encourage you to kill each other. Every life is
valued but there are some cases where people have burnt all
the rules and still use laws and rules from centuries ago where
they evade the law and trap everyone using unjust tricks in
such cases just like anyone fighting for a system change will
do. We will use any means possible to pick out just one real
culprit behind all this and show that person the power of the
brain.
There is no one with a monopoly of the brain. Things have
changed. I am going to put a fair and new system that is
respected by all and one that everyone will obey. I swear and
say to those who think a cult or other unfair institutions will
protect them after wronging others then I say think again.
Tomorrow's World Order; a new law and order. We will assign
anyone to do our work. We will write manuals which we will
publish as a deterrent and to show that there is no one above
the law.
Everything I have said above will cost nothing.
All the things you will use are MP3 or videos that are cheap
when we are fully operational.
That means the best system at no cost to anyone.
We will also be strict with those who abuse our system and

take out people just because they are rich etc. Only those who
are still doing what everyone agreed was bad like digital
slavery, genocide, killing of women and children, those still
doing digital torture and other abuses.

This means that now you can assign a drone with an explosive
to take out the culprit.
Again, I stress that this is not for everyone out there but for
those approved by Tomorrow's World Order, those who will
work for us.
Those who are to be taken out must be proved to have
committed heinous crimes against others.
I tell you once we are fully operational there are never going to
be people who will hide from us ever again. We will use your
own image to locate you and make you face justice. I tell you
sometimes when we are so advanced, we can simply sit down
and know exactly where everyone is. Those who hide behind
remote control and abuse others, those who hide in caves,
those who take other identities to hide all of you there is no
tomorrow for all you.
The only thing that will save you is doing the right thing from
now on. Justice is imminent and inevitable.
We have developed a system so advanced that it nearly
equals what the creator the mighty Yahweh does.
Yahweh knows everyone's thoughts just by looking at you.
Imagine all your thoughts and those for you were with.
This is the world's first. I can tell you that according to Yahweh
himself no one has searched for him and found him for 17
billion years. This is the first time a human being has
contacted Yahweh when he is alive [apart from the bible times]
I wrote several books about Yahweh.
Yahweh is the majestic ruler and creator of all the universe.
Yahweh knows everyone on earth and knows all your hairs.
Imagine all your hairs Yahweh knows all one by one.
So, as us.
We have become so advanced that we can just look at you
and know all your hairs, your DNA sequence, the DNA
sequence you need to stop aging, the likely death day other

things being equal.
Therefore, we are not just in the business of locating evil culprits but also of helping humanity.
But you all know that sometimes to live all together in peace means some evil going to hell.
Above all we have discovered a way to send people to hell, even alive.
Hell is real, trust me. All these warmongers who are killing women and children have never seen hell.
We have noticed that if some people die, they get stuck. Even the evilest ones. They do not go to heaven or heaven their souls get stuck.
Now we are working hard to make sure that we will send these souls to hell if they have been bad but someone from the underworld is standing on top of them without them being burnt in hell.

The best way to deal with those who hide behind technology and abuse others remotely we have put a match. Like I said earlier, there is no monopoly of the brain. The best thing is that for 99.9% of the world population all you need is your brain and one simple command.
"My voice is my password."
This is the single command you need to interact with your own brain. Your brain is the best system that has ever existed. You can ask it questions and things you do not know, and it will tell you.
For some you can actually clone yourself and send your clone to everyone even in the future or in the past as far as creation. Read all my books.

The best system that has ever existed.

Like I said our system is based on what we call Natural God Intelligence. A system that God Yahweh gave everyone the creator. All we must do is initiate the conversation with it. All you need is to understand it.

Now imagine that if humans who are better than most
computers in thinking have only 71 million DNA sequence
combinations. Above all, this DNA sequence is what makes
humans smarter than other creatures. The smartest person
among humans has a DNA sequence of 72 million.
Now picture what the creator Yahweh, God with a DNA
sequence of 53 billion and 285 million in value can do. If
intelligence is linked to your DNA sequence value, then no one
among humans compares to him.
But now know that I have managed to obtain Yahweh's DNA
sequence of 53 billion and 285 million in value.
But I am not saying that I am Yahweh no. I am not Yahweh
and I do not want to be Yahweh.
I am just saying that I solved what I call God's Dilemma. If
humans spend billions trying to create a robot like us. One that
thinks, acts, and aims to be like us. Yahweh might have
created humans to see if one of us can rise to the challenge
and walk in Yahweh's footsteps here on earth.
According to Yahweh himself. If we fail to solve life's puzzles
like what is the tree of life there is no eternity for humans.
According to him no human has managed to discover him for
17 billion years.
That means we might be doing something wrong especially
considering the number of people who bend down to worship
every day and every year.

That said, I will show you why this is the best system.

The ability to clone, resurrect and send to hell as an advantage.

Since getting God's image [some people will tell you that this
is not the case – up to you] I have discovered that I can clone
myself and other people, I can resurrect dead people and send
others to hell or heaven. But you must understand what a
person is made up of.

A person's brain has an electromagnetic brain, a soul and
another soul meaning 3 lives in one.
By the way Yahweh is three to four people in one.
Read my book series Thoughts to word or audio.

https://play.google.com/store/search?q=david%20gomadza&c
=books&hl=en_GB&gl=US

The electromagnetic wave part of the brain is the one that can
be cloned easily above all the real you. The one that will never
die given that electromagnetic waves will never be lost. They
can be absorbed and bounced off surfaces.
But a triangle can dissipate these electromagnetic waves. That
means dissolving them that is lost.
So, the opposite of being lost is being amplified or increased in
quantity and this is called electromagnetic wave eletete.
This part of the brain is the real you in terms of speech,
thinking, memory and all tasks.
The brain talks in terms of vibrations and electromagnetic
waves movement and body sequencing.
These clones are the ones that are used to locate people and
to send messages. You can simply clone yourself and send
yourself around the world.
But there are issues with people of the opposite sex as
sometimes the clone must enter the body like a ghost or the
feeling you get is that of a ghost visiting. So beat scary to
others etc.

Our system is based on what Yahweh does.

Yahweh knows everyone on earth and where the person is on
earth using what I call God's body geographical location
system.
The first time a person is created or born a reference index
number is sent to him that sticks on his body. Over the years
that position on his body represents him or her alone. If
Yahweh wants to know what you are thinking about, he simply
places his finger on his body where that person's reference is

saved and presses. Instantly he knows everything recorded by
your brain using Yahweh's time 23:90 minutes.

I can do the same as well. I can simply look at anyone's
picture and instantly if it is the first time that person's name
and reference is saved on my body. Depending on how the
brain views your feelings and his or her the first time you meet
or yours the first time you see the photo of someone. If it is
someone you love, that person will be saved near your heart
on my body. If it is an enemy, he will be saved somewhere
else like on top of the top lip on the right side of the body as
enemy.

All I must do to locate this person is to touch that place and
close my eyes. I can know the direction in which that person
is.
I can create a message and send using my brain that will
search where he or she is and ask the message to send me
the rough coordinates of that person.
But I have developed a digital analogue that will do the same.
All you need to do is to simply play the video after entering
other values which I will discuss in later volumes.

Therefore, our system is easy and cheap to use. It might not
cost you a cent.
You will need to download videos from our website
www.twofuture.world

WHO WE ARE

I am the founder of Tomorrow's World Order, a new global political organization that aims to change the current system that is based on wars. A system that is driven by wars and the killings of women and children.
I believe that the death of a child or a woman is an attack on all of us as humans.
We must do more to protect women and children especially during wars and bring the perpetrators to justice.
Do you know that women are doomed outright even before the start of a war ?

Some regimes tampering with DNA sequences over the years? Or natural evolution?
DNA sequence 620 with most people of the developed world regards women as collateral during wars.
This could be a result of tampering or evolution but nevertheless something we cannot tolerate in this day and age. Gone are the days when men kill women needlessly.
If its evolution, then we must ban these wars to protect women and children during wars.

I tell you today that unless I put in a new system , there will always be wars. This is because the system in place is fed by wars and considers wars as the drivers of the economy. To

make things worse, wars in this system have a 17 to 20 year -
cycle. That means on average after every 20 years there must
be a huge war or one war that receives weapons from most of
the leading weapons manufacturing countries.
This is embedded in the system.
There is nothing you can do today that will completely stop
wars. This is because wars correct the imbalance and prevent
a crush but act as a pressure release valve. In a system like
this stagnant growth is followed by high inflation, high
unemployment, high stockpiles of weapons and high
government debt. Years without wars means huge weapons
stockpiles and less demand but still the military will be a huge
burden for the government through salaries.
If the country cannot go to war, it must then offload its
weapons that will restart production, demand, and revive the
economy again as production of weapons increases.
In this case wars are the only real solutions to the system
either at home or abroad where your weapons are used.

This in turn has meant your leaders using past war scripts like
the Second Anglo-Dutch war of 1665-1667 to start a war
abroad following the script event by event.
We have no issues with wars as such. We stand firm against
wars that get innocent women and children killed.
Any death of a woman or child is an attack on all of us. These
people are regarded as defenseless members of society. Not
because they are women but because evolution or tampering
has meant that they are the victims where they are killed, and
everyone considers it as okay without anyone being brought
to justice.

The rescuers of people who are oppressed [e.g., the West]
Sometimes can actually go on to kill more people, most
women and children than the dictator they have toppled.
Still people talk of liberation from tyranny.
But the lives of these matter too.
Okay this is the past.
What about the future?

I will implement a new system that is based on technological advancement.
A system that is stagnant will increase the manufacturing of technology related items all with nothing to do with wars.
This is the future. I will take you all to the next stage of development. A technologically advanced stage driven by successes in technology.

We started in 2017 .
I have authored several books that will interest you.
1. Tomorrow's World Order

https://play.google.com/store/books/details/David_Gomadza_Tomorrow_s_World_Order?id=VDauDwAAQBAJ&hl=en_GB&gl=US

2. Tomorrow's World Order: A New Law & Order.: Dealing with Threats of Invasions, Wars and War Crimes

https://play.google.com/store/books/details/David_Gomadza_Tomorrow_s_World_Order_A_New_Law_Ord?id=ws3ODwAAQBAJ&hl=en_GB&gl=US

3. The New Laws
    https://play.google.com/store/books/details/David_Gomadza_The_New_Laws?id=XI2vDwAAQBAJ&hl=en_GB&gl=US

Therefore, who is Tomorrow's World Order?

We are the defenders of the defenseless innocent women and children who are killed needlessly.
We stand for all casualties of wars, even your best assets; your soldiers are protected by our laws.
We aim to put a new system of global governance and planning where we have the last overall say to things that affect all humanity.

We are not going to change your leaders etc. A big no. We do not care about country specific politics. We aim to lead the world and guide everyone in dealing with things that affect the whole of humanity. Things like climatic change, global poverty, global wars, global inequality, stagnating economies, global inflation, and all financial crises.

We are going to establish an initiative-taking government that acts in advance.
One that collects US$1 million every year from each country for stopping future wars, for dealing with the aftermaths of wars, for dealing with natural disasters like earthquakes and flooding.
The greatest challenges humanity will face will be climatic change and wars as things press. Yahweh predicted [said] harsh climatic change enough to wipe out all humans by 2084 are on the way. Humans must do whatever they can to safeguard future generations.
Do you know that the Egyptians and other people from other countries-built pyramids to control climate change?
This is true.
Imagine how much they sacrificed and even left us gold and treasure so that we are here today.
According to Yahweh there are cycles of humanity. Humans' growth is followed by harsh climatic change and destruction of all people and the beginning again of creation of people by Yahweh. The next cycle of creation according to him will start in 2084. That means if we do not act now by 2084 harsh electromagnetic waves will destroy humanity.

Take a look at the pyramids of Giza in Egypt. Ask yourself if I could be correct that the real reason why Yahweh asked them to build the pyramids was not just for the afterlife but to control climatic change. Pyramids are like triangles that dissipate electromagnetic waves. Meaning that pyramids control the forces that make the earth rotate therefore climatic change. Now check how many climatic disasters ravaged areas with pyramids? Probably not as bad as other areas.

After all these structures can be safe buildings if the earth
changes in the future as well as tourist attractions.

Therefore, talk to your leaders about my plans.

THE PROBLEM

This does not need too many explanations.

We have wars , cults, and notorious regimes and culprits who are above the law.

Do not get me wrong, I am not against wars just per se. We stand firm against wars that kill women and children. Full stop.

Destroy an innocent woman and child and one day the law will catch up with you.

We have made hunting culprits as easy as 123.

We can all start swearing by Google that it will show us your photo, the only thing we need to clone you, and use your clone to put you to sleep, in order to ambush you or for it to start the eject the body by pressing the death switch.

Therefore, these are words of advice and never threats.

We are to put a new system of global governance and planning and law and order is paramount to its success.

We as well must stand firm to evil.

These are words of advice to those thinking they can get away by going underground or use digital technology to still conduct banned practices like slavery , torture, genocide and trigger needless wars to cream other people's souls to use as attacking weapons etc.

All this is a thing of the past.

See how easy it is to locate anyone on earth by a simple picture image search.

Evil, think twice.

Dig a pit and spit in it and change or change will change you. Ladies and gentlemen welcome to Tomorrow's World Order Visit www.twofuture.world

27

THE FUTURE OF WARFARE

How will future wars be fought?
With guns and drones and still sacrificing your best boys and
girls in soldiers?
Still sacrificing women and children?

How about cloning ourselves and letting them fight for
whatever grievances we have and save humans?
We can shift from sacrificing our best for stupid land etc and
let us start to value the lives of good people.
We can fight electromagnetic wave clone wars.
Let us all value women and children and start a new era when
there are no wars.
Welcome to Tomorrow's World Order

ABOUT DAVID GOMADZA

I am the first global president of the world.

Visit www.twofuture.world